JIMI HENDRIX

A Musician's Collection

The status of Jimi Hendrix as the definitive guitar player is well documented in other publications. This collection has been put together for ALL musicians attracted to Jimi's compositions. They are presented here in standard Piano/Vocal/Guitar format. It is an excellent source book that provides a unique perspective of his music.

All interior black and white photos by: JOSEPH SIA

Color photography: ED CARAEFF

Photo research: BILL NITOPI

ISBN 0-7935-0419-8

Exclusively Distributed by
Hal Leonard Publishing Corporation
7777 West Bluemound Road P.O. Box 13819 Milwaukee, WI 53213

AIN'T NO TELLING

Words and Music by
JIMI HENDRIX

BOLD AS LOVE

Words and Music by
JIMI HENDRIX

ALL ALONG THE WATCHTOWER

Words and Music by
BOB DYLAN

14

BURNING OF THE MIDNIGHT LAMP

Words and Music by
JIMI HENDRIX

CAN YOU SEE ME

Words and Music by
JIMI HENDRIX

Can you hear _

CASTLES MADE OF SAND

Words and Music by
JIMI HENDRIX

CROSSTOWN TRAFFIC

Words and Music by
JIMI HENDRIX

EZY RIDER

Words and Music by
JIMI HENDRIX

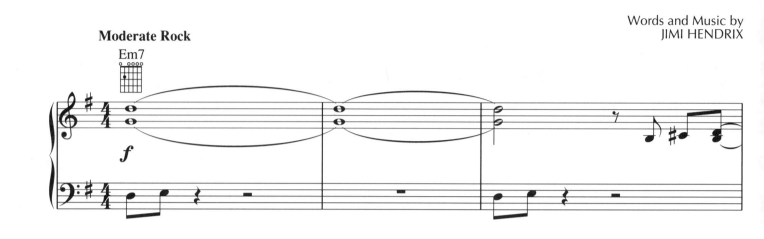

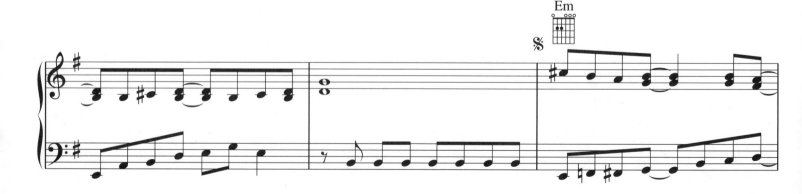

How long do you think he's gon-na last?_

Can I fore-cast? See all the lov-ers say, do what you please.

FIRE

By JIMI HENDRIX

Repeat and Fade

FOXY LADY

Words and Music by
JIMI HENDRIX

I wan-na take you home,
I'm gon-na take you home,
yeah,

I won't do you no harm.___ You've got to be all

mine, all mine. Ooh, fox-y la-dy.

Fox-y.

pre-cious time.___ You've got to be all mine, all mine.

Foxy lady.

Foxy Foxy.

D.S. al Coda

CODA

Guitar Tacet

Foxy lady, comin' and get-cha.

Repeat and Fade

GYPSY EYES

Words and Music by
JIMI HENDRIX

Well, I re - al - ize that I've been hyp - no - tized.__ I love you

gyp - sy eyes._____ I love you gyp - sy eyes._____

To Coda

___ Well al - right.

men fight-in' to the death o - ver me to - day. __ I'll

try to meet cha by the old high - way. _____ Hey!

no chord
D.C. al Coda

CODA

__ I love you gyp-sy __ eyes. _____

I love you gyp - sy — eyes. _____

Well, al - right.

and   I   been   saved. _____

Oh, ___   I   been   saved. _

Am

That's why I   love you.   Said I

Repeat and Fade

love   you.   Hey!

HAVE YOU EVER BEEN
(TO ELECTRIC LADYLAND)

Words and Music by
JIMI HENDRIX

Moderately slow

Have you ev - er been, _____ have you ev - er been _ to E -

lec - tric La - dy - land? _ The ma - gic car - pet waits _

for you _ so don't you be late. _____ Oh, I I wan - na

HEY JOE

Words and Music by
BILLY ROBERTS

Moderately Slow Rock

Hey, _____ Joe, _____ uh where you go - in' with that gun in your hand? Hey, _____ Joe, I said where you goin' with that gun in your hand? _____ Al - right.

HOUSE BURNING DOWN

Words and Music by
JIMI HENDRIX

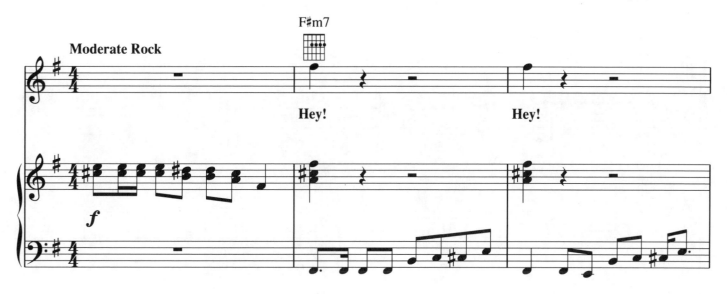

F#m   **E**   **D**   **Esus**

Down   down   down.

Em7

D#m7

Well, I asked my friend, "Where is that
Well, some - one stepped from the crowd. He was

Em7   **G#m7**   **Am**

black smoke com-in' from?" He just coughed and changed the sub-ject and said, "Uh, I
nine - teen miles high. She shouts re - tired and dis-gust - ed so we paint

81

IF 6 WAS 9

Words and Music by
JIMI HENDRIX

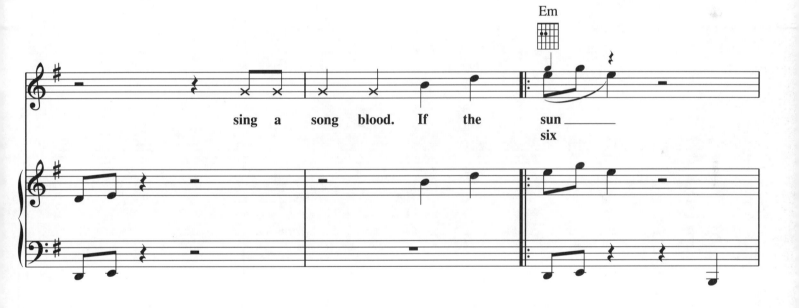

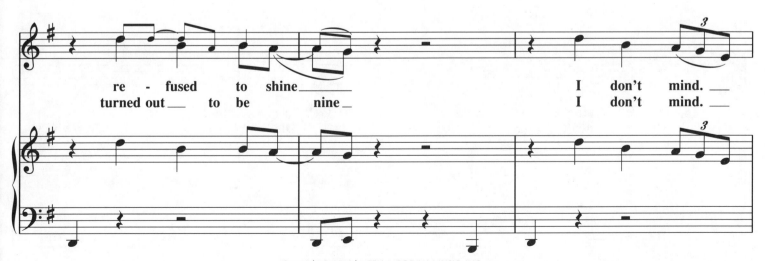

84

Em7/A

Dm7/G

E

Wave on,   wave on.

Repeat and Fade

KILLING FLOOR

Words and Music by
CHESTER BURNETT

LITTLE WING

Words and Music by
JIMI HENDRIX

LITTLE MISS LOVER

Words and Music by
JIMI HENDRIX

F7#9

Hey, hey, Lit - tle Miss Lov - er. Well now a

so much you and me can dis - cov - er. but I think we should start.

LOVE OR CONFUSION

Words and Music by
JIMI HENDRIX

Is that the stars _____ in the sky _____ or is

con - fu - sion?_____   Ma-ma, we   must get to-geth-er__ and

uh   find out

ex - act - ly what we're tryin' to do.

Love __   or con - fu - sion?

LONG HOT SUMMER NIGHT

Words and Music by
JIMI HENDRIX

MANIC DEPRESSION

Words and Music by
JIMI HENDRIX

Repeat as needed

MAY THIS BE LOVE

Words and Music by
JIMI HENDRIX

Wa - ter - fall, _____ don't ev - er change _____

your ways. _____ Fall with me

for a ____ mil - lion ____ days. Oh, my wa - ter -

fall.

Repeat and Fade

PURPLE HAZE

Words and Music by
JIMI HENDRIX

RED HOUSE

Words and Music by
JIMI HENDRIX

REMEMBER

Words and Music by
JIMI HENDRIX

SPANISH CASTLE MAGIC

Words and Music by
JIMI HENDRIX

STONE FREE

By JIMI HENDRIX

Stone free, don't try to o-pen that.

Stone free, I'm mov-in' on down the high-way. Yeah,

stone free, got-ta got-ta got-ta got-ta. Stone free, oh yeah.

F(no3rd)

Bye - bye, ba - by. Stone free.

UP FROM THE SKIES

Words and Music by
JIMI HENDRIX

If my dad-dy could see me now.

WAIT UNTIL TOMORROW

Words and Music by
JIMI HENDRIX

WILD THING

Words and Music by
CHIP TAYLOR

THE WIND CRIES MARY

Words and Music by
JIMI HENDRIX

foot-prints dressed in red. ___ And the wind ___ whis-pers

Mar - y. ___ A broom is drear-i - ly ___ sweep-ing ___

___ up the brok-en piec - es of yes-ter-day's life.

Some - where ___ a queen ___ is weep - ing. ___ Some-